가장 알기 쉽게 배우는

초등

기초 영어회화 구어체 기본문장수록

기본영어

STEP BY STEP BOOK 1(입문)

가장 알기 쉽게 배우는

초등 기본 영어
STEP BY STEP BOOK 1(입문)

저 자 방정인
발행인 고본화
발 행 반석출판사
2020년 6월 15일 초판 1쇄 인쇄
2020년 6월 20일 초판 1쇄 발행
홈페이지 www.bansok.co.kr
이메일 bansok@bansok.co.kr
블로그 blog.naver.com/bansokbooks

07547 서울시 강서구 양천로 583. B동 1007호
　　　　(서울시 강서구 염창동 240-21번지 우림블루나인 비즈니스센터 B동 1007호)
대표전화 02) 2093-3399 **팩 스** 02) 2093-3393
출 판 부 02) 2093-3395 **영업부** 02) 2093-3396
등록번호 제315-2008-000033호

ISBN 978-89-7172-917-5 (63740)

가장 알기 쉽게 배우는

초등

기본영어

기초 영어 회화 구 어체 기본문장 수록

STEP BY STEP BOOK 1(입문)

반석출판사
Bansok

머리말

국제 개방 시대를 맞아 생활 영어회화의 필요성은 날로 증대하고 있습니다.

초·중학교 영어 교육 방향이 문법과 독해 위주에서 회화 위주의 교육으로 방향 전환되었습니다. 더욱이 1996년부터 초등학교에 영어가 정규 과목으로 채택되면서 초등학교 영어는 회화 위주로 교육되고 있습니다.

문법은 영어를 효율적으로 배우는 데 필요한 과정의 한 부분입니다. 영어 교육은 읽고 내용을 파악할 능력을 갖춘 후, 영어를 듣고 자기의 의사를 상대방에게 정확히 전달할 수 있는 능력을 갖추게 해야 합니다.

그런데 그동안의 영어 교육은 영어를 듣고 말할 수 있는 능력을 교육하지 못했습니다. 그래서 앞으로 영어회화를 효율적이고 성공적으로 교육하기 위해서는 교육 프로그램과 교사의 영어회화 능력을 증진시켜야겠습니다. 가장 중요한 것은 우리나라 학생들에게 알맞은 영어회화 교재와 교육 방법의 출현입니다. 그동안 거의 모든 영어회화 교재는 성인을 위한 내용으로 일관되어 있었습니다.

반석출판사에서는 초등학생을 위한 생활 영어회화 교재인 『초등 기본 영어 STEP BY STEP』을 저술하게 되었습니다.

『초등 기본 영어 STEP BY STEP BOOK 1』(입문)은 영어회화 기초로서 구어체 중심으로 실생활 영어를 수록하였습니다. 초등학생을 위한 기초 영어회화 교재로 구성하였습니다.

『초등 기본 영어 STEP BY STEP BOOK 2』(문형)은 『초등 기본 영어 STEP BY STEP BOOK 1』(입문)을 기초로 대화의 폭을 넓혔습니다. 『초등 기본 영어 STEP BY STEP BOOK 1』(입문)을 마치거나 수준 높은 학생을 위하여 초등학생들의 생활상을 다루었습니다.

영어 듣기와 영어 말하기의 성공을 위해서는 Native Speaker와 회화 공부를 하는 것도 좋지만 현실적으로 가장 이상적인 방법은 음원을 활용한 회화교육입니다. 회화교육도 반복 교육만이 유일한 길입니다.

끝으로 『초등 기본 영어 STEP BY STEP』을 통해 영어회화 교육에 성공하기를 기원하는 바입니다.

저자 방정인

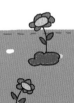

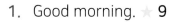

목차

목차

목 차

이 책의 특징

이 책은 전체가 99과로 구성되어 있습니다. 과가 너무 많은가요? 그렇지만 걱정하지 마세요. 차근차근 공부하다 보면 어느새 99과가 훌쩍 지나가 있을 테니까요. 전체 99과는 총 11과씩 9개의 큰 덩어리로 이루어져 있답니다.

11개의 과들은 총 8개의 짧은 대화들과 1개의 노래, 1개의 행동으로 옮기기 그리고 1개의 복습으로 이루어져 있어요. 어린이는 먼저 5개의 짧은 대화들을 공부하게 돼요. 재미있는 그림과 함께 있는 짧은 대화들은 인사부터 시작해서 묻고 답하기까지 다양하게 구성되어 있어요. 특히 책에 함께 담긴 mp3 CD나 음원과 함께 공부할 경우 먼저 대화를 듣고 나중에 따라 읽게 되어 있어서 듣기와 말하기/읽기 연습을 고르게 할 수 있어요. 하나의 대화가 끝난 다음에는 앞에서 배운 대화에 바꾸어 넣기 연습을 해볼 수 있게 되어 있어요.

5개의 대화들을 공부한 후, 어린이는 영어 노래를 하며 잠시 쉬어갈 수 있어요. 책에 실린 악보를 보며 부모님, 선생님, 형/오빠, 누나/언니, 동생들과 함께 영어로 된 재미있는 노래를 불러 보세요. 노래로 힘을 충전한 후에는 3개의 대화를 금방 공부할 수 있을 거예요.

그 다음으로는 그림을 보며 영어를 듣고 행동으로 옮기는 신체활동을 해볼 수 있어요. 신체활동과 함께 영어를 공부함으로써 어린이는 영어를 몸으로도 익힐 수 있게 될 거예요.

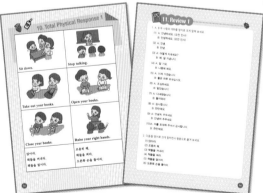

마지막으로는 앞에서 공부한 대화들을 영어로 말해보기, 주어진 한글을 영어로 말하면서 행동으로 옮겨보기의 두 파트로 구성된 복습을 하게 될 거예요. 복습을 통해서 어린이는 자신이 익힌 영어회화를 다시 한 번 기억해서 말해볼 수 있게 돼요.

한꺼번에 많이 공부를 해도 되지만, 하루에 한 과씩 공부를 해 볼 수도 있어요. 그 날 배운 영어회화를 부모님이나 형제들, 혹은 친구들과 함께 연습해 보세요. 실제 대화로 구성되어 있기 때문에 어렵지 않게 익힐 수 있을 거랍니다. 자, 그럼 풍성한 영어회화의 세계로 빠져들어 볼까요?

1. Good morning.

A: Good morning.
B: Good morning.

A: 안녕하세요.
B: 안녕하세요.

 SUBSTITUTION DRILLS

Good <u>morning.</u>
(1) afternoon
(2) evening

 1. Good morning. (안녕하세요.) ·································· (오전 인사)
2. Good afternoon. (안녕하세요.) ·························· (오후 인사)
3. Good evening. (안녕하세요.) ···························· (저녁 인사)
   만났을 때의 인사로 Good morning.으로 인사하면 Good morning.으로 답례
한다.

2. Hi!

A: Hi.
B: Hello.

A: 안녕.
B: 안녕.

SUBSTITUTION DRILLS

A: Hi.
B: <u>Hello.</u>
  (1) Hi

해설 1. A: Hi.   B: Hi.
2. A: Hello.   B: Hello.
3. A: Hello.   B: Hi.
오전, 오후, 저녁 상관없이 아무 때나 만났을 때 젊은이들 사이에 자주 쓰이는
인사이다.
Hi.로 인사하면 Hi. 또는 Hello.로 인사한다.

3. How are you?

3

A: How are you?
B: Fine, thank you.

A: 어떻게 지내세요?
B: 예, 잘 지냅니다.

 SUBSTITUTION DRILLS

A: How are you?
B: <u>Fine,</u> thank you.
   (1) Very well
   (2) Pretty good

 어떻게 지내느냐 안부를 물을 때 쓰이는 말이다. 대답은 자기의 건강이나 기분 상태를 말해준다.

4. Good bye.

A: Good bye.
B: See you.

A: 잘 가요.
B: 나중에 봐요.

 SUBSTITUTION DRILLS

A: Good bye.
B: <u>See you.</u>
   (1) Good bye.   (2) Bye.
   (3) So long.   (4) See you again.

해설 헤어질 때 쓰이는 인사말로 Good bye. 대신에 Bye. / So long, / See you (later, again). 등이 쓰인다. See you.는 See you later.를 줄여서 쓰는 말이다.

5. I'm going now.

A: I'm going now.
B: Have a nice day.

A: 이제 가겠습니다.
B: 좋은 하루 보내십시오.

 SUBSTITUTION DRILLS

A: <u>I'm going now.</u>
B: <u>Have a nice day.</u>

   A: (1) I have to go now.   (2) I should be leaving now.
   B: (1) Have a good day.   (2) Have a nice trip.

 I have to go now.: 지금 가야 한다.
have to = must: ~해야 한다
I should be leaving now.: 지금 떠나야 하겠다.
Have a nice trip.: 좋은 여행 되세요. 잘 가세요.

6. Song

Twinkle, Twinkle, Little Star

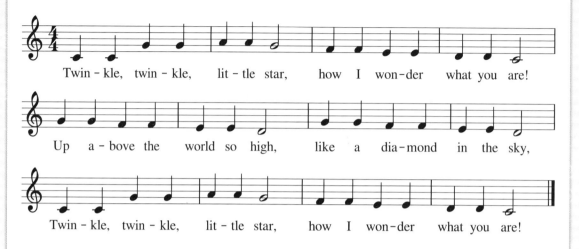

Twinkle, twinkle, little star, how I wonder what you are!
Up above the world so high, like a diamond in the sky,
Twinkle, twinkle, little star, how I wonder what you are!

7. Be careful.

A: Be careful.
B: Okay.

A: 조심하세요.
B: 알았습니다.

SUBSTITUTION DRILLS

A: <u>Be careful.</u>
B: <u>Okay.</u>

    A: (1) Take it easy.   (2) Take care.   (3) Look out.
    B: (1) You, too.   (2) Thanks.   (3) Don't worry.

 Take it easy.: 조심하세요. 살펴가세요. 편히 마음을 가지세요. 등의 뜻이 있다.
Take care.: 조심해.
Look out.: 위험해.

8. I'm home.

A: I'm home.
B: Come on in.

A: 다녀왔습니다.
B: 들어와라.

SUBSTITUTION DRILLS

A: <u>I'm home.</u>
B: <u>Come on in.</u>

    A: (1) I'm back.   (2) I've just come home.
    B: (1) Please come in.   (2) How was it today?

 I'm home.이나 I'm back.은 집에 이미 와 있는 상태를 말하며, I've just come home.은 막 도착한 모습을 나타낸다. How was it today?는 오늘 어떤 상태였나를 묻는 말이다.

9. Thank you.

A: Thank you.
B: You're welcome.

A: 감사합니다.
B: 천만에요.

SUBSTITUTION DRILLS

A: <u>Thank you.</u>
B: <u>You're welcome.</u>

    A: (1) Thanks.   (2) Thank you for inviting me.
    B: (1) Not at all.   (2) Don't mention it.

 '천만에요.'라는 뜻으로 주로 You're welcome.이 쓰인다. 영국식 표현으로 Don't mention it.도 쓰인다. 강한 뜻으로 Not at all.도 쓰인다.

10. Total Physical Response 1

Sit down.

Stop talking.

Take out your books.

Open your books.

Close your books.

Raise your right hands.

앉아라.	조용히 해.
책들을 꺼내라.	책들을 펴라.
책들을 덮어라.	오른쪽 손을 들어라.

1. A, B 두 사람의 대화를 영어로 크게 말해 보세요.

(1) A: 안녕하세요. (오전 인사)
    B: 안녕하세요. (오전 인사)

(2) A: 안녕.
    B: 안녕.

(3) A: 어떻게 지내세요?
    B: 예, 잘 지냅니다.

(4) A: 잘 가요.
    B: 나중에 봐요.

(5) A: 이제 가겠습니다.
    B: 좋은 하루 보내십시오.

(6) A: 조심하세요.
    B: 알았습니다.

(7) A: 다녀왔습니다.
    B: 들어와라.

(8) A: 감사합니다.
    B: 천만에요.

(9) A: 안녕히 주무세요.
    B: 안녕히 주무세요.

(10) A: 저를 초대해 주셔서 감사합니다.
     B: 천만에요.

2. 다음을 영어로 크게 말하면서 행동으로 옮겨 보세요.

(1) 앉아라.
(2) 조용히 해.
(3) 책들을 꺼내라.
(4) 책들을 펴라.
(5) 책들을 덮어라.
(6) 오른쪽 손을 들어라.

12. Excuse me.

A: Excuse me.
B: That's okay.

A: 실례합니다.
B: 괜찮습니다.

SUBSTITUTION DRILLS

A: Excuse me.
B: <u>That's okay.</u>
    (1) Yes. May I help you?   (2) What can I do for you?
    (3) All right.   (4) Can I help you?

 Excuse me.의 대답으로 All right.(괜찮습니다.)를 쓰며 무엇을 도와줄까를 상대
방에게 물어보는 것도 예의이다.

13. Hurry up!

A: Hurry up!
B: Wait!

A: 서둘러!
B: 기다려!

12
—
13

 SUBSTITUTION DRILLS

A: Hurry up!
B: Wait!

   A: (1) Hurry, hurry.   (2) Don't hurry.
   B: (1) Wait a minute.   (2) Okay.

 Wait!은 Wait a minute.를 줄여서 쓰는 말이다.
Hurry up! / Hurry, hurry. 등은 '서둘러라'라는 명령문으로 쓰인다.

14. Listen.

A: Listen.
B: What?

A: 들어봐.
B: 뭘?

SUBSTITUTION DRILLS

A: <u>Listen.</u>
B: <u>What?</u>

   A: (1) Listen to me.   (2) Look at me.
   B: (1) What did you say?   (2) Who?

 Listen to me.: 내 말에 귀를 기울여라.
What? = What is it?의 준말이다.
look at: ~을 보다

15. Be quiet!

A: Be quiet!
B: I'm sorry.

A: 조용히 해!
B: 미안합니다.

SUBSTITUTION DRILLS

A: <u>Be quiet!</u>
B: <u>I'm sorry.</u>

    A: (1) Stop talking.   (2) Quiet down.   (3) Shut up.
    B: (1) Yes, sir.   (2) Yes, ma'am.   (3) Okay.

 Be quiet. / Silence! / Quiet down. / Stop talking. / Don't make a noise. 등은 떠들지 말라는 뜻이고, Shut up.은 '닥쳐'라는 뜻을 가진 심한 표현이다.

16. I'm hungry.

A: I'm hungry.
B: Me, too.

A: 배고파.
B: 나도 배고파.

SUBSTITUTION DRILLS

A: I'm hungry.

B: <u>Me, too.</u>

(1) I'm full. (2) I'm not.

(3) Will you have any hamburgers? (4) Let's go to eat hamburgers.

 Me, too. = I'm hungry, too.의 준말이다.
배부르다는 뜻으로 I'm full. 혹은 I had enough. 등을 사용한다.

17. Song

Yankee Doodle

Yankee Doodle went to town upon a little pony,
He stuck a feather in his cap and called it macaroni.
Yankee Doodle, Doodle Doo, Yankee Doodle Dandy,
All the lassies are so smart and sweet as sugar candy.

Father and I went down to camp along with captain good in
And there we saw the men and boys eat thick and tasty pudding.
Yankee Doodle keep it, Yankee Doodle Dandy.
Mind the music and the stepping with the girls being handy.

18. Ouch!

A: Ouch!
B: Are you all right?

A: 아야!
B: 괜찮니?

SUBSTITUTION DRILLS

A: Ouch!
B: <u>Are you all right?</u>
   (1) You hurt your leg.   (2) Muscleache?
   (3) Swollen?   (4) Does it hurt?

해설 muscleache: 근육통   cramp: 경련
        stomachache: 복통   headache: 두통
        backache: 요통   sore: 쓰린
        swollen(Is it swollen?): 부은
        painful: 아픈

19. Oops!

A: Oops!
B: What's the matter?

A: 저런!(아이고!)
B: 무슨 일이에요?

SUBSTITUTION DRILLS

A: Oops!

B: <u>What's the matter?</u>

(1) Are you all right?   (2) What happened?

(3) Are you okay?   (4) Look out!

 Oops: 아이고! 저런!(놀람이나 당황을 나타내는 소리)

Look out! = Watch out!: 위험해!(조심해!) 머리 위로 무엇인가 떨어질 때 혹은
어떤 위험이 닥칠 때 위험을 알리는 소리

20. Oh, no!

A: I forgot.
B: Oh, no!

A: 잊어버렸어.
B: 설마!(그럴 리가!)

SUBSTITUTION DRILLS

A: <u>I forgot.</u>

B: Oh, no!

   (1) His sister married.   (2) He passed the exam.

   (3) I finished the work.   (4) We did it.

 Oh, no.: 설마, 그럴 리가, 안 돼, 끔찍해 등 놀라움을 나타내는 소리이다.
We did it.: 고생 끝에 어떤 일을 해냈을 때 기뻐서 얼싸안고 소리치는 소리이다.

Stand up, Min-jae.

Come to the front.

Erase the blackboard.

Bring some chalk.

Write your name on the board.

Go back to your seat.

민재야, 일어서.	앞으로 나와.
칠판을 지워라.	분필을 좀 가져와라.
칠판에 네 이름을 써라.	네 자리로 돌아가라.

1. A, B 두 사람의 대화를 영어로 크게 말해 보세요.

   (1) A: 실례합니다.
       B: 괜찮습니다.

   (2) A: 서둘러!
       B: 기다려!

   (3) A: 들어봐.
       B: 뭘?

   (4) A: 조용히 해!
       B: 미안합니다.

   (5) A: 배고파.
       B: 나도 배고파.

   (6) A: 아야!
       B: 괜찮니?

   (7) A: 저런!
       B: 무슨 일이에요?

   (8) A: 잊어버렸어.
       B: 설마!

   (9) A: 아야!
       B: 부었어?

   (10) A: 저런!
        B: 괜찮아?

2. 다음을 영어로 크게 말하면서 행동으로 옮겨 보세요.

   (1) 민재야, 일어서.
   (2) 앞으로 나와.
   (3) 칠판을 지워라.
   (4) 분필을 좀 가져와라.
   (5) 칠판에 네 이름을 써라.
   (6) 네 자리로 돌아가라.

23. Give me that.

A: Give me that.
B: Here you are.

A: 저것 주세요.
B: 여기 있습니다.

SUBSTITUTION DRILLS

A: <u>Give me that.</u>
B: <u>Here you are.</u>

    A: (1) Show me that.   (2) Show me another.

        (3) Can you show me that one?

    B: (1) Here it is.   (2) Yes, of course.

        (3) Yes, ma'am.

 물건을 내주면서 Here you are. / Here it is. 등의 표현을 사용한다.
자기 마음에 들지 않을 때 Show me another.를 사용한다.

24. Are you ready?

A: Are you ready?
B: Not yet.

A: 준비됐어?
B: 아니, 아직.

SUBSTITUTION DRILLS

A: <u>Are you ready?</u>

B: <u>Not yet.</u>

   A: (1) Are you finished?   (2) Are you leaving?

      (3) Are you busy?

   B: (1) No, I'm not.   (2) Not yet.

      (3) Yes, I am.

 Not yet.: I am not ready yet.의 준말이다.

Are you leaving? 여기에서 〈be + 현재분사(동사-ing)〉는 미래의 뜻이 있다.

32

25. Whose turn?

A: Whose turn?
B: My turn.

A: 누구 차례니?
B: 내 차례야.

SUBSTITUTION DRILLS

A: <u>Whose turn?</u>
B: <u>My turn.</u>

    A: (1) Your bag?   (2) His skates?   (3) Her shoes?
    B: (1) Yes, it's mine.   (2) No, they aren't.   (3) Yes, they are.

 Whose turn? = Whose turn is it?의 준말이다.
My turn. = It is my turn.의 준말이다.
Your bag? = Is this[that] your bag?
His skate? = Are these[those] his skates?

26. Can I?

A: Can I?
B: Go ahead.

A: ~해도 될까요?
B: 해!(어서!)

SUBSTITUTION DRILLS

A: <u>Can I?</u>
B: <u>Go ahead.</u>

   A: (1) May I?   (2) May I?
   B: (1) Yes, of course.   (2) No, you may not.

 Can I? Can I _____? 뒤에 말이 생략되어 있다. 일종의 허락을 구하는 말이다.
Go ahead. = Ahead.: 요청에 대한 허락을 나타내는 말이다.

27. Really?

A: Really?
B: Of course.

A: 그래?(어머!)
B: 물론.(그래!)

SUBSTITUTION DRILLS

A: Really?
B: <u>Of course.</u>

(1) Sure.   (2) That's right.

(3) She got first prize at the piano contest.   (4) My sister got married.

 해설 Really?는 상대방의 말에 대해서 감탄사적으로 어머! / 그래? / 아니! 등으로 쓰이고, 그렇지 않을 때는 정말? 과연? 등으로 쓰인다.

28. Song

I've been Working on the Railroad

I've been working on the railroad all the live-long day,
I've been working on the railroad to pass the time away.
Don't you hear the whistle blow-in'? Rise up so early in the morn.
Don't you hear the cap'n shout-in'? "Dinah, blow your horn."

29. Congratulations.

A: We won the baseball game.
B: Congratulations.

A: 야구 경기에 승리했어.
B: 축하합니다.

SUBSTITUTION DRILLS

A: <u>We won the baseball game.</u>
B: Congratulations.
    (1) I passed the examination.   (2) I did it.
    (3) We arrived at the South Pole.   (4) I finished the computer program.

 어떤 일을 성취했을 때 축하하는 말로 Congratulations.를 쓴다. 이때 s를 꼭 뒤
에 붙여야 한다.
I did it.은 고생이나 분투 끝에 어떤 일을 완성했을 때 환호하는 말이다.

30. What's up?

A: What's up?
B: I feel blue.

A: 왜 그래?(무슨 일인데?)
B: 우울해.

SUBSTITUTION DRILLS

A: <u>What's up?</u>

B: <u>I feel blue.</u>

    A: (1) What's the matter?   (2) What's wrong?

    B: (1) I'm hurt.   (2) I've been feeling down lately.

해설 What's up? = What is up?: 걱정되어 묻는 말로서 '왜 그러냐? / 무슨 일이냐?' 라는 뜻이다.

I'm blue.: blue는 파란색이 아니라 우울할 때 혹은 기분이 좋지 않을 때 쓰이는 말이다.

31. I'm sorry.

A: I'm sorry.
B: That's all right.

A: 미안합니다.
B: 괜찮습니다.

SUBSTITUTION DRILLS

A: I'm sorry.
B: <u>That's all right.</u>

    (1) No problem.   (2) Never mind.

    (3) That's okay.   (4) It doesn't matter.

해설 That's all right.: 괜찮습니다.
No problem.: 전혀 문제가 되지 않아요.
Never mind.: 걱정하지 마세요.
That's okay.: 괜찮아요.
It doesn't matter.: 걱정 마세요.

Stand up, Hyun-woo.

Walk to the door.

Open the door and go out.

Go to the teacher's room.

Bring an eraser and some chalk.

Put them on the desk.

현우야, 일어서.	문으로 걸어가.
문을 열고 밖으로 나가라.	교무실로 가라.
지우개와 분필 좀 가져와라.	그것들을 책상에 놓아라.

1. A, B 두 사람의 대화를 영어로 크게 말해 보세요.

(1) A: 저것 주세요.

B: 여기 있습니다.

(2) A: 준비됐어?

B: 아니, 아직.

(3) A: 누구 차례니?

B: 나 차례야.

(4) A: ~해도 될까요?

B: 해.(어서)

(5) A: 그래?

B: 물론.

(6) A: 야구 경기에 승리했어.

B: 축하합니다.

(7) A: 왜 그래?(무슨 일인데?)

B: 우울해.

(8) A: 미안합니다.

B: 괜찮습니다.

(9) A: 무슨 일이야?

B: 다쳤어.

(10)A: 우린 해냈어.

B: 축하해.

2. 다음을 영어로 크게 말하면서 행동으로 옮겨 보세요.

(1) 현우야, 일어서.

(2) 문으로 걸어가.

(3) 문을 열고 밖으로 나가라.

(4) 교무실로 가라.

(5) 지우개와 분필 좀 가져와라.

(6) 그것들을 책상 위에 놓아라.

34. You look pale.

A: You look pale.
B: I've been feeling down lately.

A: 창백해 보여.
B: 요즘 계속 기분이 좋지 않아.

SUBSTITUTION DRILLS

A: <u>You look pale.</u>
B: <u>I've been feeling down lately.</u>

   A: (1) You look happy.   (2) You look blue.
      (3) You look beautiful.
   B: (1) Thank you.   (2) My friend died.
      (3) Thanks a lot.

 〈You look + 형용사〉가 오면 얼굴의 표정을 나타낼 수 있다.
pale: 창백한 blue: 우울한 feel down에서 down은 기분이 내려앉으니까 전체적으로 기분이 좋지 않은 것을 의미한다.

35. Leave me alone.

A: Can I help you?
B: Leave me alone.

A: 내가 도와줄까?
B: 내버려 둬.

SUBSTITUTION DRILLS

A: <u>Can I help you?</u>
B: <u>Leave me alone.</u>

   A: (1) May I help you?   (2) How can I help you?
      (3) Can I help you?

   B: (1) Yes, please.   (2) Don't worry about me.
      (3) Don't bother me.

 상대방이 호의를 보일 때 거절하는 말로 Leave me alone. / Don't worry about me. / Don't bother me. 등이 있다. 호의를 받아들일 때에는 Yes, please. / Thank you. 등이 있다.

43

36. Who?

A: Stand up.
B: Who?

A: 일어서.
B: 누구?

SUBSTITUTION DRILLS

A: <u>Stand up.</u>

B: <u>Who?</u>

  A: (1) Sit down.   (2) Come here.

     (3) Answer the questions.

  B: (1) Me?   (2) Who, me?

     (3) Him?

 Who? = Who do you mean?

Me?나 Him? 대신에 I?나 He?는 사용하지 않는다.

Me? = Is it me?   Him = Is it him?

44

37. Me, neither.

A: I don't like it.
B: Me, neither.

A: 난 그것을 좋아하지 않아.
B: 나도 좋아하지 않아.

SUBSTITUTION DRILLS

A: <u>I don't like it.</u>
B: <u>Me, neither.</u>

   A: (1) I like it.   (2) I don't know.   (3) I have to go.
   B: (1) Me, too.   (2) Me, neither.   (3) Me, too.

 Me, neither. = I don't like it, either.
Me, too. = I like it, too.
He likes it. - I like it, too. -〉 긍정문에는 too
He doesn't like it. - I don't like it, either. -〉 부정문에는 either

38. That's too bad.

A: I have a cold.
B: That's too bad.

A: 감기 걸렸어요.
B: 안됐군요.

SUBSTITUTION DRILLS

A: <u>I have a cold.</u>
B: <u>That's too bad.</u>

    A: (1) He's down with the flu.   (2) I feel dizzy.
    B: (1) I'm sorry to hear that.   (2) Since when?

해설 That's too bad.: 상대방의 상태가 좋지 않으면 동정의 뜻으로 자주 쓰이는 말이다.

I'm sorry to hear that.: 그 말을 들으니 유감스럽다.

I feel dizzy.: 어지럽다

39. Song

Old MacDonald Had a Farm

Old Mac - Don - ald   had   a   farm,   Ee - igh, ee - igh,

oh!   And   on   this   farm   he   had   some   chicks.

Ee - igh, ee - igh,   oh!   With a   chick, chick   here,   (and a)

chick chick there,   Here a chick, there a chick,   ev - ery-where a chick, chick.

Old   Mac - Don - ald   had   a   farm,   Ee - igh, ee - igh,   oh!

Old MacDonald had a farm, Eeigh eeigh, oh!

And on this farm he had some chicks, Eeigh, eeigh, oh!

With a chick, chick here, and a chick chick there,

Here a chick, there a chick, everywhere a chick, chick.

Old MacDonald had a farm, Eeigh, eeigh, oh!

Old MacDonald had a farm, Eeigh, eeigh, oh!

And on this farm he had some ducks, Eeigh, eeigh, oh!

With a quack, quack here, and a quack, quack there;

Here a quack, there a quack, everywhere a quack, quack,

Old MacDonald had a farm, Eeigh, eeigh, oh!

40. Cheer up!

A: I don't feel like trying again.
B: Cheer up!

A: 다시 하고 싶지 않아.
B: 힘내!

SUBSTITUTION DRILLS

A: <u>I don't feel like trying again.</u>

B: Cheer up!

(1) I failed in the examination.

(2) I can't play baseball today.

(3) I didn't get first prize at the English Speech Contest.

(4) I missed the bus.

해설 Cheer up!은 상대가 절망이나 실의에 빠졌을 때 용기를 내라는 말이다.
feel like + 동명사: ~하고 싶다

41.Come on. Let's go together.

A: Come on. Let's go together.
B: That's great.

A: 자, 함께 가자.
B: 그것 참 좋네요.

SUBSTITUTION DRILLS

A: <u>Come on. Let's go together.</u>
B: <u>That's great.</u>

    A: (1) Come on. Toss me the ball.   (2) Come on. Hit me.
    B: (1) Okay. Never mind.   (2) Sure. I will.

 Come on.: 자. 상대편에게 재촉하는 말이다.
That's great.: 찬성의 뜻으로 쓰인다.
Never mind.: 걱정 마. 안심해.

42. Look. It's bleeding.

A: Look. It's bleeding.
B: Stay calm. It's not serious.

A: 큰일 났어. 피가 나.
B: 침착해. 별것 아니야.

SUBSTITUTION DRILLS

A: <u>Look. It's bleeding.</u>
B: <u>Stay calm. It's not serious.</u>

   A: (1) Look. Your leg is swollen.   (2) Oh! What's the matter?
   B: (1) That's all right. I'm not in pain.   (2) I just hurt my foot.

해설 Look.: 봐!(큰일 났어!)
Stay calm.: 침착해.(가만있어.)
I'm not in pain.: 아프지 않다
What's the matter?: 무슨 일이야?

Come to the blackboard.

Draw an apple on the board.

Write the words 'an apple' under the picture.

Read the words aloud three times.

Erase the picture and the words.

Go back to your seat and sit down.

칠판으로 와라.

그림 밑에 '사과' 낱말을 써라.

그림과 낱말을 지워라.

칠판에 사과를 그려라.

그 낱말을 크게 세 번 읽어라.

네 자리로 가서 앉아라.

44. Review 4

1. A, B 두 사람의 대화를 영어로 크게 말해 보세요.

  (1) A: 창백해 보여.
      B: 요즘 계속 기분이 좋지 않아.

  (2) A: 내가 도와줄까?
      B: 내버려 둬.

  (3) A: 일어서.
      B: 누구?

  (4) A: 난 그것을 좋아하지 않아.
      B: 나도 좋아하지 않아.

  (5) A: 감기 걸렸어요.
      B: 안됐군요.

  (6) A: 어지러워요.
      B: 언제부터?

  (7) A: 다시 하고 싶지 않아.
      B: 힘내!

  (8) A: 자, 함께 가자.
      B: 그것 참 좋네요.

  (9) A: 큰일 났어. 피가 나.
      B: 침착해. 별것 아니야.

  (10) A: 이리 와.
      B: 지민이에요?

2. 다음을 영어로 크게 말하면서 행동으로 옮겨 보세요.

  (1) 칠판으로 와라.
  (2) 칠판에 사과를 그려라.
  (3) 그림 밑에 '사과' 낱말을 써라.
  (4) 그 낱말을 크게 세 번 읽어라.
  (5) 그림과 낱말을 지워라.
  (6) 네 자리로 가서 앉아라.

45. Is this a map?

A: Is this a map?
B: Yes, it is.

A: 이것은 지도입니까?
B: 예, 그렇습니다.

SUBSTITUTION DRILLS

1. A: Is <u>this</u> a map?
   B: Yes, it is.
       (1) that   (2) it
2. A: Is this <u>a map</u>?
   B: Yes, it is.
       (1) a picture   (2) a calendar

해설 This is a map. (긍정문)
Is this a map? (의문문)
this로 묻든, that으로 묻든, it으로 묻든 대답은 모두 it으로 한다.

46. Is that a desk?

A: Is that a desk?
B: No, it isn't. It's a table.

A: 저것은 책상입니까?
B: 아니오, 그렇지 않습니다. 그것은 탁자입니다.

SUBSTITUTION DRILLS

A: Is that <u>a desk</u>?
B: No, it isn't. It's <u>a table</u>.

A: (1) a chair   (2) a pencil
   (3) a notebook   (4) a window
B: (1) a bench   (2) a pen
   (3) an album   (4) a door

해설 Yes 다음에는 반드시 긍정문이 쓰이고, No 다음에는 반드시 부정문이 쓰인다.
isn't는 is not의 준말이다.

A: Are you a student?
B: Yes, I am.

A: 당신은 학생입니까?
B: 예, 그렇습니다.

SUBSTITUTION DRILLS

A: <u>Are you</u> a student?
B: Yes, <u>I am</u>.

A: (1) Is he	(2) Is she
(3) Is your brother	(4) Is your sister
B: (1) he is	(2) she is
(3) he is	(4) she is

 you로 물으면 I로, he로 물으면 he로, she로 물으면 she로, 남자로 물으면 he로, 여자로 물으면 she로 대답한다. I am / You are / He is / She is 등처럼 be동사의 쓰임이 다르다.

48. Are you a doctor?

A: Are you a doctor?
B: No, I'm not. I'm a teacher.

A: 당신은 의사입니까?
B: 아니오, 그렇지 않습니다. 나는 교사입니다.

SUBSTITUTION DRILLS

A: Are you <u>a doctor</u>?
B: No, I'm not. I'm <u>a teacher</u>.

A: (1) American	(2) Japanese
(3) French	(4) Chinese

B: (1) English	(2) Korean
(3) German	(4) Thai

해설 America – American   England – English   Japan – Japanese
Korea – Korcan   France – French   China – Chinese
Germany – German   Thailand – Thai

A: Do you have a cap?
B: Yes, I do.

A: 모자를 가지고 있습니까?
B: 예, 그렇습니다.

SUBSTITUTION DRILLS

A: <u>Do you</u> have a cap?

B: Yes, <u>I do</u>.

    A: (1) Does he   (2) Does she

       (3) Does Tom   (4) Does Jane

    B: (1) he does   (2) she does

       (3) he does   (4) she does

 have동사나 일반동사의 의문문은 현재형에서 Do나 Does로 질문하고, 간단한 대답은 do나 does로 대답한다.

Do you go to school? – Yes, I do.   Does he go to school? – Yes, he does.

50. Song

We Wish You a Merry Christmas

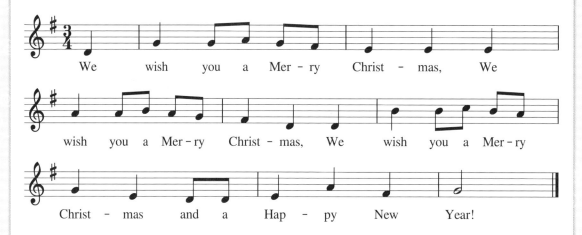

We wish you a Merry Christmas, We wish you a Merry Christmas,
We wish you a Merry Christmas, And a Happy New Year!

Let's all do a little clapping, Let's all do a little clapping,
Let's all do a little clapping, And spread Christmas cheer.

We wish you a Merry Christmas, We wish you a Merry Christmas,
We wish you a Merry Christmas, And a Happy New Year!

Let's all do a little jumping, Let's all do a little jumping,
Let's all do a little jumping, And spread Christmas cheer.

We wish you a Merry Christmas, We wish you a Merry Christmas,
We wish you a Merry Christmas, And a Happy New Year!

Let's all do a little twirling, Let's all do a little twirling,
Let's all do a little twirling, And spread Christmas cheer.

We wish you a Merry Christmas, We wish you a Merry Christmas,
We wish you a Merry Christmas, And a Happy New Year!

51. Does he study English?

A: Does he study English?
B: No, he doesn't. He studies Chinese.

A: 그는 영어를 공부합니까?
B: 아니오, 그렇지 않습니다. 그는 중국어를 공부합니다.

 SUBSTITUTION DRILLS

A: Does he <u>study English</u>?
B: No, he doesn't. He <u>studies Chinese</u>.

A: (1) have a car   (2) study Japanese   (3) walk to school
B: (1) has a bike   (2) studies Korean   (3) goes to school by bus

 He studies English. (긍정문)
He doesn't study English. (부정문)
don't는 do not의 준말이고 doesn't는 does not의 준말이다.

52. Can you speak Korean?

A: Can you speak Korean?
B: Yes, I can.

A: 한국말을 할 수 있습니까?
B: 예, 할 수 있습니다.

SUBSTITUTION DRILLS

A: Can you speak <u>Korean</u>?
B: <u>Yes, I can</u>.

    A: (1) English   (2) Japanese
    B: (1) No, I can't.   (2) No, I can't. I can speak Chinese.

 조동사와 be동사의 의문문과 부정문은 묻고 대답하는 방법이 같다.
일반동사와 have동사의 의문문과 부정문은 묻고 대답하는 방법이 같다.

53. Will you open the door?

A: Will you open the door?
B: Yes, I will.

A: 문을 열어주시겠습니까?
B: 예. 그렇게 하지요.

SUBSTITUTION DRILLS

A: <u>Will you open the door?</u>

B: <u>Yes, I will.</u>

   A: (1) Will you bring me the bag? (2) Will you close the window?

   B: (1) No, I won't.   (2) Yes, of course.

 Will you open the door?는 상대방의 의사를 들으면서 상대방에게 해줄 것을 요구하는 문형이다. 대답에는 Yes와 No가 있다.

Take out your notebooks.

Write the numbers from one to ten in them.

Count them aloud two times.

Put a circle around the number nine.

Show your notebook to your teacher.

Close your notebooks.

노트를 꺼내라.

그 숫자를 크게 두 번 읽어라.

선생님께 네 노트를 보여드려라.

그 노트에 1에서 10까지 숫자를 써라.

숫자 9에 동그라미를 그려 넣어라.

노트를 덮어라.

1. A, B 두 사람의 대화를 영어로 크게 말해 보세요.

  (1) A: 이것은 지도입니까?
       B: 예, 그렇습니다.

  (2) A: 저것은 책상입니까?
       B: 아니오, 그렇지 않습니다. 그것은 탁자입니다.

  (3) A: 당신은 학생입니까?
       B: 예, 그렇습니다.

  (4) A: 당신은 의사입니까?
       B: 아니오, 그렇지 않습니다. 나는 교사입니다.

  (5) A: 모자를 가지고 있습니까?
       B: 예, 그렇습니다.

  (6) A: 그는 영어를 공부합니까?
       B: 아니오, 그렇지 않습니다. 그는 중국어를 공부합니다.

  (7) A: 한국말을 할 수 있습니까?
       B: 예, 할 수 있습니다.

  (8) A; 문을 열어주시겠습니까?
       B: 예, 그렇게 하지요.

  (9) A: 저에게 가방을 가져다주시겠습니까?
       B: 아니, 싫은데요.

  (10)A: 창문을 열어주시겠습니까?
       B: 예, 물론이지요.

2. 다음을 영어로 크게 말하면서 행동으로 옮겨 보세요.

  (1) 노트를 꺼내라.
  (2) 그 노트에 1에서 10까지 숫자를 써라.
  (3) 그 숫자를 크게 두 번 읽어라.
  (4) 숫자 9에 동그라미를 그려 넣어라.
  (5) 선생님께 네 노트를 보여 드려라.
  (6) 노트를 덮어라.

56. Shall I close the window?

A: Shall I close the window?
B: Yes, please.

A: 창문을 닫아 드릴까요?
B: 예, 부탁합니다.

SUBSTITUTION DRILLS

A: <u>Shall I close the window?</u>

B: <u>Yes, please.</u>

    A: (1) Can I carry your bag?

       (2) Should I take you to your mother?

    B: (1) No, thank you.

       (2) Yes, take me to my mother.

 미국에서는 Shall I ~? 대신에 Can I ~? 혹은 Should I ~? 등이 많이 사용되는 경향이 있다. 위의 표현은 상대방에게 물을 때 자기가 하겠다는 의사를 나타내는 말이다.

A: Shall we meet at eight in the evening?
B: Yes, let's meet then.

A: 저녁 8시에 만날까요?
B: 예, 그때 만납시다.

SUBSTITUTION DRILLS

A: <u>Shall we meet at eight in the evening?</u>
B: <u>Yes, let's meet then.</u>

    A: (1) Should we go on a picnic?   (2) Can we sing together?
    B: (1) No, let's not do that.   (2) Yes, let's do that.

 미국에서는 Shall we ~? 대신에 Should we ~? 혹은 Can we ~? 등이 많이 사용되는 경향이 있다. 위의 표현 모두가 상대방에게 권유할 때 사용된다.

58. Shall he bring the bag?

A: Shall he bring the bag?
B: Yes, let him bring it.

A: 그에게 가방을 가져오게 할까요?
B: 예, 그에게 가져오게 하지요.

SUBSTITUTION DRILLS

A: Shall he bring the bag?

B: Yes, let him bring it.

   A: (1) Shall she write a letter to him?

      (2) Shall Tom keep his diary?

   B: (1) No, let her not write a letter.

      (2) Yes, let him keep his diary.

해설 Shall he bring the bag?과 같이 질문하면 상대방에게 그 사람에게 시킬 것인지 의사를 물어보는 것이다. 이때 대답은 Let처럼 사역동사로 한다.

59. May I have ice cream?

A: May I have ice cream?
B: Yes, you may.

A: 아이스크림을 먹어도 되나요?
B: 예, 좋아요.

SUBSTITUTION DRILLS

A: <u>May I have ice cream?</u>
B: <u>Yes, you may.</u>

    A: (1) May I play with the doll?   (2) May I have some coffee?

    B: (1) No, you may not.   (2) No, you must not.

 해설 May I have ice cream?에서 May I ~?로 물어보면 긍정일 경우 Yes, you may.로 대답하고 부정일 경우 No, you may not.(약한 금지) / No, you must not.(강한 금지)으로 대답한다. 최근에 미국에서는 No, you must not.은 잘 쓰이지 않는다.

60. Do I have to learn English?

A: Do I have to learn English?
B: Yes, you have to.

A: 제가 영어를 배워야 하나요?
B: 예, 그렇습니다.

SUBSTITUTION DRILLS

A: <u>Do I have to learn English?</u>

B: <u>Yes, you have to.</u>

    A: (1) Do I have to stay at home all day?

        (2) Do I have to go home now?

    B: (1) No, you don't have to.

        (2) Yes, you have to.

 Must I ~?는 Do I have to ~?로, Yes, you must.는 Yes, you have to.로, No, you need not.은 No, you don't have to.로 쓰인다.

61. Song

Head, Shoulders, Knees and Toes

Head, shoulders, knees and toes, knees and toes,
Head, shoulders, knees and toes, knees and toes,
And eyes, and ears, and mouth and nose,
Head, shoulders, knees and toes, knees and toes.

62. Would you like some milk?

A: Would you like some milk?
B: Yes, please.

A: 우유 좀 드시겠어요?
B: 예, 좋습니다.

SUBSTITUTION DRILLS

A: <u>Would you like some milk?</u>

B: <u>Yes, please.</u>

    A: (1) Would you like to sing a song?

        (2) Would you like some tea?

    B: (1) Yes, I'd like to.

        (2) No, thank you.

해설 Would you like some milk?로 물으면 Yes, I would. / Yes, please. / Yes, thank you. / No, I wouldn't. / No, thank you. / No, I just drank some. 등으로 대답할 수 있다.

63. May I speak to Jane?

62
63

A: May I speak to Jane?
B: This is Jane speaking.

A: 제인 바꿔 주세요.
B: 제인인데요.

 SUBSTITUTION DRILLS

A: <u>May I speak to Jane?</u>
B: <u>This is Jane speaking.</u>
   A: (1) I'd like to speak to Min-jae.
      (2) Can I speak to Hyun-woo?
  B: (1) Min-jae speaking.
     (2) Hold on, please.

 전화를 바꿔달라는 말로 May[Can] I speak to Jane? / I'd like to speak to Jane. 등이 있다. 본인이 받았을 때는 Speaking. / That's me. / This is he[she]. 등으로 대답한다.

64. Hello! I'd like to speak to Hyun-woo.

A: Hello! I'd like to speak to Hyun-woo.
B: He's on another phone. Who's calling, please?

A: 여보세요! 현우 좀 바꿔주세요.
B: 다른 전화를 받고 있는데요. 누구시지요?

SUBSTITUTION DRILLS

A: <u>Hello! I'd like to speak to Hyun-woo.</u>

B: <u>He's on another phone. Who's calling, please?</u>

   A: (1) Hello. Is this 855-6364?

       (2) Hello! Can I speak to Ji-min?

   B: (1) Sorry, wrong number.

       (2) She's out. Call her again later.

 통화중일 때 The line is busy. 다른 전화와 통화중일 때 He is on another phone.
/ He's talking on another line. 등으로 말할 수 있다. Wrong number.는 전화가
잘못 걸렸을 때 할 수 있는 대답이다.

Touch your head.

Touch your nose.

Clap your hands three times.

Stomp your foot five times.

Spin around seven times.

Sit down.

머리를 만져라.

손뼉을 세 번 쳐라.

일곱 번 뱅글 돌아라.

코를 만져라.

발을 다섯 번 세게 굴러라.

앉아라.

66. Review 6

1. A, B 두 사람의 대화를 영어로 크게 말해 보세요.

   (1) A: 창문을 닫아 드릴까요?
       B: 예, 부탁합니다.

   (2) A: 저녁 8시에 만날까요?
       B: 예, 그때 만납시다.

   (3) A: 그에게 가방을 가져오게 할까요?
       B: 예, 그에게 가져오게 하지요.

   (4) A: 아이스크림을 먹어도 되나요?
       B: 예, 좋아요.

   (5) A: 제가 영어를 배워야 하나요?
       B: 예, 그렇습니다.

   (6) A: 우유 좀 드시겠어요?
       B: 예, 좋습니다.

   (7) A: 제인 바꿔주세요.
       B: 제인인데요.

   (8) A: 여보세요! 현우 좀 바꿔주세요.
       B: 다른 전화를 받고 있는데요. 누구시지요?

   (9) A: 민재 좀 바꿔주세요.
       B: 외출하였는데요. 후에 다시 전화 주세요.

   (10)A: 여보세요. 855-6343인가요?
       B: 미안하지만 잘못 거셨습니다.

2. 다음을 영어로 크게 말하면서 행동으로 옮겨 보세요.

   (1) 머리를 만져라.
   (2) 코를 만져라.
   (3) 손뼉을 세 번 쳐라.
   (4) 발을 다섯 번 세게 굴러라.
   (5) 일곱 번 뱅글 돌아라.
   (6) 앉아라.

67. What's this?

A: What's this?
B: It's a blackboard.

A: 이것은 무엇입니까?
B: 그것은 칠판입니다.

SUBSTITUTION DRILLS

A: <u>What's this?</u>
B: <u>It's a blackboard.</u>

    A: (1) What's that?   (2) What's this?
    B: (1) It's a map.   (2) It's a picture.

 의문사로 물으면 Yes나 No로 대답하지 않고 뒤를 내려 읽는다. this나 that으로 물으면 it으로 대답한다.
What's this? = What is this?

68. What's your name?

A: What's your name?
B: My name is Eun Kyoung.

A: 당신의 이름은 무엇입니까?
B: 나의 이름은 은경입니다.

SUBSTITUTION DRILLS

A: <u>What's your name?</u>
B: <u>My name is Eun Kyoung.</u>

    A: (1) Who are you?   (2) Your name, please.
    B: (1) I'm Eun Kyoung.   (2) My name is Hana.

해설 이름을 물어볼 때 몇 가지 표현이 있다.
What's your name? – My name is Ji-min.
Who are you? – I'm Ji-min.
May I ask your name? – My name is Ji-min.

69. Where's your mother?

A: Where's your mother?
B: My mother's in the kitchen.

A: 엄마 어디 계시니?
B: 엄마 부엌에 계세요.

SUBSTITUTION DRILLS

A: <u>Where's your mother?</u>

B: <u>My mother's in the kitchen.</u>

    A: (1) Where's your father?   (2) Where's her apartment?

    B: (1) He's at his office.   (2) It's in Jamsil.

 where로 물으면 장소를 나타내는 부사구로 대답한다. 좁은 장소는 at, 넓은 장소는 in을 주로 사용한다.

70. Where are you from?

A: Where are you from?
B: I'm from Seoul, Korea.

A: 어디서 왔니?
B: 한국, 서울에서 왔어.

SUBSTITUTION DRILLS

A: <u>Where are you from?</u>
B: <u>I'm from Seoul, Korea.</u>

    A: (1) Where are you from?   (2) Where did you come from?

    B: (1) I'm from New York.   (2) I came from Tokyo.

 어디서 왔느냐의 표현으로 Where are you from? / Where did you come from? 등이 있지만 주로 Where are you from?이 많이 쓰인다.

71. When's your birthday?

A: When's your birthday?
B: My birthday is September 16th.

A: 당신의 생일은 언제입니까?
B: 나의 생일은 9월 16일입니다.

SUBSTITUTION DRILLS

A: <u>When's your birthday?</u>

B: <u>My birthday is September 16th.</u>

    A: (1) When's your lunch time?

       (2) When's your mother's birthday?

    B: (1) It's at twelve-thirty.

       (2) Her birthday is August 24th.

 When으로 물어보면 때를 나타내는 부사구를 사용하여 대답한다.

Bingo

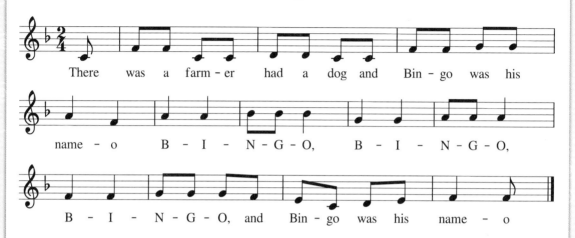

There was a farm-er had a dog and Bin-go was his name-o B-I-N-G-O, B-I-N-G-O, B-I-N-G-O, and Bin-go was his name-o

There was a farmer had a dog
And Bingo was his name-o
B-I-N-G-O, B-I-N-G-O,
B-I-N-G-O,
And Bingo was his name-o

A: How's the weather?
B: It's fine.

A: 날씨가 어때요?
B: 날씨가 좋아요.

SUBSTITUTION DRILLS

A: <u>How's the weather?</u>
B: <u>It's fine.</u>

A: (1) How's the weather?　　　(2) How's your father?
B: (1) It's rainy[cloudy].　　　(2) He's fine.

 How로 물으면 주로 상대방의 상태나 현재의 상황을 나타낸다.
fine은 날씨나 사람의 상태가 좋을 때 쓰인다.

74. Why were you absent yesterday?

A: Why were you absent yesterday?
B: Because I was sick.

A: 넌 어제 왜 결석했니?
B: 아팠기 때문이에요.

SUBSTITUTION DRILLS

A: <u>Why were you absent yesterday?</u>

B: <u>Because I was sick.</u>

    A: (1) Why are you late?

       (2) Why are you sleepy?

    B: (1) Because I got up late.

       (2) Because I slept for only two hours.

해설 시제에는 현재, 과거, 미래가 있다. am-was, is-was, are-were, get-got, sleep-slept 등으로 동사의 현재가 과거로 변한다.
Because를 생략할 때가 많다.

75. What time is it now?

A: What time is it now?
B: It is six o'clock.

A: 지금은 몇 시입니까?
B: 6시입니다.

SUBSTITUTION DRILLS

A: What time is it now?

B: <u>It is six o'clock.</u>

    (1) It's six-thirty.   (2) It's half past six.

    (3) It's a quarter past six.   (4) It's five to six.

해설 6시: It's six o'clock.

6시 30분: It's six thirty. / It's half past six.

6시 15분: It's six fifteen. / It's a quarter past six.

6시 5분 전: It's five to six.

Bring the box.

Open the box.

Take out one apple.

Eat the apple.

Show a big smile.

Go back to your seat and sit down.

상자를 가져와라.	상자를 열어라.
사과 하나를 꺼내라.	사과를 먹어라.
함박미소를 지어라.	네 자리로 가서 앉아라.

77. Review 7

1. A, B 두 사람의 대화를 영어로 크게 말해 보세요.

(1) A: 이것은 무엇입니까?
B: 그것은 칠판입니다.

(2) A: 당신의 이름은 무엇입니까?
B: 나의 이름은 은경입니다.

(3) A: 엄마 어디 계시니?
B: 엄마 부엌에 계세요.

(4) A: 어디서 왔니?
B: 한국, 서울에서 왔어.

(5) A: 당신의 생일은 언제입니까?
B: 나의 생일은 9월 16일입니다.

(6) A: 날씨가 어때요?
B: 날씨가 좋아요.

(7) A: 넌 어제 왜 결석했니?
B: 아팠기 때문이에요.

(8) A: 지금은 몇 시입니까?
B: 6시입니다.

(9) A: 지금 몇 시죠?
B: 12시 30분인데요.

(10) A: 아빠 어디 계시니?
B: 사무실에 계셔.

2. 다음을 영어로 크게 말하면서 행동으로 옮겨 보세요.

(1) 상자를 가져와라.
(2) 상자를 열어라.
(3) 사과 하나를 꺼내라.
(4) 사과를 먹어라.
(5) 함박미소를 지어라.
(6) 네 자리로 가서 앉아라.

78. What day is it today?

A: What day is it today?
B: It is Sunday today.

A: 오늘은 무슨 요일입니까?
B: 오늘은 일요일입니다.

SUBSTITUTION DRILLS

A: <u>What day is it today?</u>

B: <u>It is Sunday today.</u>

    A: (1) What day is it tomorrow?

       (2) What day was it yesterday?

    B: (1) It's Monday tomorrow.

       (2) It was Saturday yesterday.

해설 What day is it today?라고 질문하면 날짜를 묻는 것이 아니라 요일을 묻는 것이다.

86

79. What's the date today?

A: What's the date today?
B: It's September 16th.

A: 오늘은 며칠입니까?
B: 9월 16일입니다.

SUBSTITUTION DRILLS

A: What's the date today?
B: It's September 16th.
    (1) It's January 27th.   (2) It's March 25th.
    (3) It's August 24th.   (4) It's May 14th, 2020.

 날짜를 물어볼 때에는 What's the date?로 표현한다.
요일을 물어볼 때에는 What day is it?으로 표현한다.

78
—
79

80. How old are you?

A: How old are you?
B: I'm ten years old.

A: 너 몇 살이니?
B: 나 10살이야.

SUBSTITUTION DRILLS

A: <u>How old are you?</u>

B: <u>I'm ten years old.</u>

   A: (1) How tall are you?

      (2) How much is this computer?

  B: (1) I'm five feet tall.

      (2) It's two million won.

해설 나이, 키, 거리, 가격 등을 물어볼 때에는 〈How + 형용사〉로 표현한다.
나이, 키, 거리, 넓이 등을 대답힐 때 형용사를 문미에 쓰는 것이 좋다.

81. What are you doing now?

A: What are you doing now?
B: I'm reading a story book.

A: 넌 지금 무엇을 하고 있니?
B: 난 이야기책을 읽고 있어.

SUBSTITUTION DRILLS

A: <u>What are you doing now?</u>
B: <u>I'm reading a story book.</u>
   A: (1) What is he doing now?
      (2) What's she doing now?
   B: (1) He's playing the piano.
      (2) She's playing with a doll.

 현재진행형: ⟨be + 동사-ing⟩의 형태이다. 동작의 진행을 나타내는 말이다.

82. Where are they playing the game?

A: Where are they playing the game?
B: They are playing the game in the classroom.

A: 그들은 어디에서 게임을 하고 있습니까?
B: 그들은 교실에서 게임을 하고 있습니다.

SUBSTITUTION DRILLS

A: <u>Where are they playing the game?</u>
B: <u>They are playing the game in the classroom.</u>

  A: (1) Where is Tom learning Korean?
  　 (2) Where are you studying English?
  B: (1) He's learning Korean at Bansok.
  　 (2) I'm studying English at school.

 진행형: 동작의 계속을 나타낸다. 〈be + 현재분사〉의 형태이다.
현재분사 민드는 법: 〈동사 + −ing〉이다.

83. Song

The Sun is Shining

The sun is shining the sky is blue. What are you going to do?
The sun is shining the sky is blue. What are you going to do?
I'm going to sit in the garden. And look at the sun.
I'm going to have lunch at half past one.
I'm going to write a letter to you.
I'm going to post it at half past two.

The sun is shining the sky is blue. What are you going to do?
The sun is shining the sky is blue. What are you going to do?
I'm going to run. And jump into the sea.
I'm going to swim at half past three.
I'm going to open my windows and open my door.
I'm going to have tea at half past four.

84. When are you leaving Seoul?

A: When are you leaving Seoul?
B: I'm leaving Seoul next week.

A: 언제 서울을 떠날 예정입니까?
B: 다음 주에 서울을 떠날 예정입니다.

SUBSTITUTION DRILLS

A: <u>When are you leaving Seoul?</u>

B: <u>I'm leaving Seoul next week.</u>

  A: (1) When will you come home?

  (2) When is he arriving here?

  B: (1) I'll come home around seven.

  (2) He's arriving here soon.

해설 왕래발착동사(go, come, leave, arrive 등)는 진행형이 미래의 뜻을 나타낸다.
He is arriving here soon. = He will arrive here soon.

85. How many brothers do you have?

A: How many brothers do you have?
B: I have two.

A: 형제가 몇 있습니까?
B: 둘 있습니다.

SUBSTITUTION DRILLS

A: <u>How many brothers do you have?</u>
B: <u>I have two.</u>

    A: (1) How much money do you need?

        (2) How many hamburgers did he eat?

    B: (1) I need ten dollars.

        (2) He ate three.

 셀 수 있는 명사는 many를, 셀 수 없는 명사는 much를 사용한다.
do[does] – did / eat – ate

86. What can I do for you?

A: What can I do for you?
B: I'm just looking around.

A: 무엇을 도와드릴까요?
B: 단지 구경하고 있을 뿐입니다.

SUBSTITUTION DRILLS

A: <u>What can I do for you?</u>

B: <u>I'm just looking around.</u>

    A: (1) May I help you?   (2) Can I help you?

    B: (1) Yes, please.   (2) I'm looking for a nice hat.

 사람이 찾아오면 보통 What can I do for you? / May I help you? / Can I help you? 등으로 물어본다.

Take this box.

Show me the top of the box.

Touch the bottom of the box.

Open the box.

Show me the inside of the box.

Put the lid down.

이 상자를 집어라.	상자 꼭대기를 보여 주어라.
상자 밑바닥을 만져 보아라.	상자를 열어라.
상자 속을 보여 달라.	뚜껑을 닫아라.

88. Review 8

1. A, B 두 사람의 대화를 영어로 크게 말해 보세요.

   (1) A: 오늘은 무슨 요일입니까?
       B: 오늘은 일요일입니다.

   (2) A: 오늘은 며칠입니까?
       B: 9월 16일입니다.

   (3) A: 너 몇 살이니?
       B: 나 10살이야.

   (4) A: 넌 지금 무엇을 하고 있니?
       B: 난 이야기책을 읽고 있어.

   (5) A: 그들은 어디에서 게임을 하고 있습니까?
       B: 그들은 교실에서 게임을 하고 있습니다.

   (6) A: 언제 서울을 떠날 예정입니까?
       B: 다음 주에 서울을 떠날 예정입니다.

   (7) A: 형제가 몇 있습니까?
       B: 둘 있습니다.

   (8) A: 무엇을 도와드릴까요?
       B: 단지 구경하고 있을 뿐입니다.

   (9) A: 돈이 얼마 필요합니까?
       B: 10달러 필요합니다.

  (10) A: 그는 언제 이곳에 도착할 예정입니까?
       B: 그는 이곳에 곧 도착할 것입니다.

2. 다음을 영어로 크게 말하면서 행동으로 옮겨 보세요.

   (1) 이 상자를 집어라.
   (2) 상자 꼭대기를 보여 주어라.
   (3) 상자 밑바닥을 만져 보아라.
   (4) 상자를 열어라.
   (5) 상자 속을 보여 달라.
   (6) 뚜껑을 닫아라.

89. How does your sister get to school?

A: How does your sister get to school?
B: She goes to school by bus.

A: 당신의 여동생은 무엇을 타고 학교에 갑니까?
B: 여동생(그녀)은 버스로 학교에 갑니다.

SUBSTITUTION DRILLS

A: How does your sister get to school?
B: She goes to school by bus.

  (1) She walks to school.

  (2) She goes to school by subway.

  (3) She goes to school by school bus.

  (4) Her father drives her to school.

 교통수단은 주로 〈by + 교통수단〉으로 표현한다. 물어볼 때에는 How를 사용한다.

90. Is there a piano in the classroom?

A: Is there a piano in the classroom?
B: Yes, there is.

A: 교실에 피아노가 있습니까?
B: 예, 있습니다.

SUBSTITUTION DRILLS

A: <u>Is there a piano in the classroom?</u>

B: <u>Yes, there is.</u>

    A: (1) Is there anyone here?   (2) Are there any flowers in the garden?

    B: (1) Just a minute.   (2) No, there aren't any.

 There is + 단수명사: ~이 있습니다
There are + 복수명사: ~이 있습니다
some: 긍정문에 쓰인다.
any: 의문문과 부정문에 쓰인다.

91. How many students are there in your class?

A: How many students are there in your class?
B: There are twenty-five students.

A: 당신의 반에는 몇 명의 학생이 있습니까?
B: 25명의 학생이 있습니다.

SUBSTITUTION DRILLS

A: <u>How many students are there in your class?</u>
B: <u>There are twenty-five students.</u>

   A: (1) How much water is there in the pool?
   B: (1) There's not much in it.

 many: 많은(수) / a few: 약간의(수) / few: 거의 없는(수)
much: 많은(양) / a little: 약간의(양) / little: 거의 없는(양)

92. What are you going to do tomorrow?

A: What are you going to do tomorrow?
B: I'm going to make a model airplane.

A: 내일 너는 무엇을 할 예정이니?
B: 난 모형 비행기를 만들 예정이야.

SUBSTITUTION DRILLS

A: What are you going to do tomorrow?

B: <u>I'm going to make a model airplane.</u>

   (1) I'm going to read a poem.

   (2) I'm going to write in my diary.

   (3) I'm going to study Chinese.

   (4) I'm going to teach him English.

해설 〈be going to + 동사원형〉: ~할 예정이다, ~할 작정이다(가까운 미래를 나타낸다.) 현재진행형도 왕래발착의 동사는 미래를 대용한다.

A: Would you like to play baseball with us?
B: Yes, I'd like to.

A: 우리와 야구할래요?
B: 예, 하겠습니다.

SUBSTITUTION DRILLS

A: Would you like <u>to play baseball with us?</u>
B: Yes, I'd like to.
(1) to go on a picnic tomorrow
(2) to have some ice cream
(3) to play with us
(4) to take a walk

 to부정사가 동사의 목적어로 사용되었다. 명사적 용법으로 쓰였다.

94. Song

Jingle Bells

Dash - ing through the snow, one horse o - pen sleigh,

Over the fields we go, Laugh - ing all the way

Bells on bob - tail ring, Mak - ing spir - its bright; What

fun it is to ride and sing a sleigh - ing song to - night.

Jin - gle bells! Jin - gle bells! Jin - gle all the way!

Oh! What fun it is to ride in a one horse o - pen sleigh, hey!

Jin - gle bells! Jin - gle bells! Jin - gle all the way!

Oh! What fun it is to ride in a one horse o - pen sleigh!

Dashing through the snow, in a one horse open sleigh,
Over the fields we go, Laughing all the way.
Bells on bob tail ring, Making spirits bright;
What fun it is to ride and sing a sleighing song tonight.
Jingle bells! Jingle bells! Jingle all the way!
Oh! What fun it is to ride in a one horse open sleigh, hey!
Jingle bells! Jingle bells! Jingle all the way!
Oh! What fun it is to ride in a one horse open sleigh!

95. It's time to go to school.

A: It's time to go to school.
B: I have to hurry up.

A: 학교에 갈 시간이다.
B: 서둘러야겠다.

SUBSTITUTION DRILLS

A: <u>It's time to go to school.</u>
B: <u>I have to hurry up.</u>

A: (1) It's time to have lunch. (2) I have something to tell you.
B: (1) Let's have lunch. (2) Go ahead.

 명사 뒤에서 명사를 수식하는 to부정사의 형용사적 용법이다. '~할, ~하는'으로 해석한다.

96. I'm going to the library to read some books.

A: Where are you going?
B: I'm going to the library to read some books.

A: 넌 어디에 가고 있니?
B: 난 책 좀 읽기 위해서 도서관에 가고 있어.

SUBSTITUTION DRILLS

A: Where are you going?

B: <u>I'm going to the library to read some books.</u>

   (1) I'm going to the subway station to take the train.

   (2) I'm going to the supermarket to buy something for a school
     picnic.

 to부정사에서 부사적 용법으로 목적을 나타내는 용법은 '~하기 위하여, ~하려
고'로 해석한다.

97. I'm glad to see you.

A: How do you do?
B: I'm glad to see you.

A: 처음 뵙겠습니다.
B: 만나서 반갑습니다.

 SUBSTITUTION DRILLS

A: How do you do?
B: <u>I'm glad to see you.</u>
  (1) I'm happy to meet you.
  (2) I'm surprised to see you.
  (3) I'm pleased to meet you.
  (4) How do you do?

 처음 만났을 때의 인사말로 How do you do? 하면 How do you do? 그 다음에
는 Glad to meet you.로 답한다. 이때 to부정사는 원인을 나타낸다.

Close your books.

Put all of your things in your bags.

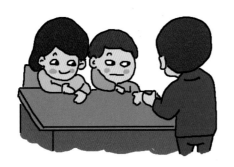

Clean your desks.

Stand up.

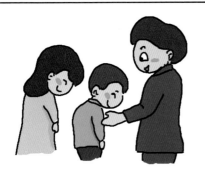

Say 'Good-bye' to your teacher.

Go out of the classroom and go home.

책들을 덮어라. 책상들을 깨끗이 치워라. 선생님께 '작별인사'를 해라.	모든 것들을 가방 안에 넣어라. 일어서라. 교실에서 나가 집으로 가라.

1. A, B 두 사람의 대화를 영어로 크게 말해 보세요.

(1) A: 당신의 여동생은 무엇을 타고 학교에 갑니까?

B: 여동생(그녀)은 버스로 학교에 갑니다.

(2) A: 교실에 피아노가 있습니까?

B; 예, 있습니다.

(3) A: 당신의 반에는 몇 명의 학생이 있습니까?

B: 25명의 학생이 있습니다.

(4) A: 내일 너는 무엇을 할 예정이니?

B: 난 모형 비행기를 만들 예정이야.

(5) A: 우리와 야구할래요?

B: 예, 하겠습니다.

(6) A: 학교에 갈 시간이다.

B: 서둘러야겠다.

(7) A: 넌 어디에 가고 있니?

B: 난 책 좀 읽기 위해서 도서관에 가고 있어.

(8) A: 처음 뵙겠습니다.

B: 만나서 반갑습니다.

(9) A: 점심 먹을 시간이다.

B: 점심을 먹자.

(10) A: 풀장에 물이 얼마나 있니?

B: 약간 있어.

2. 다음을 영어로 크게 말하면서 행동으로 옮겨 보세요.

(1) 책들을 덮어라.

(2) 모든 것들을 가방 안에 넣어라.

(3) 책상들을 깨끗이 치워라.

(4) 일어서라.

(5) 선생님께 '작별인사'를 해라.

(6) 교실에서 나가 집으로 가라.

1. A, B 두 사람의 대화를 영어로 크게 말해 보세요.

(1) **A** Good morning.
    B Good morning.
(2) **A** Hi.
    B Hi. (Hello.)
(3) **A** How are you?
    B Fine, thank you.
(4) **A** Good bye.
    B See you.
(5) **A** I'm going now.
    B Have a nice day.
(6) **A** Be careful.
    B Okay.
(7) **A** I'm home.
    B Come on in.
(8) **A** Thank you.
    B You're welcome.
(9) **A** Good night.
    B Good night.
(10) **A** Thank you for inviting me.
    B Not at all.

2. 다음을 영어로 크게 말하면서 행동으로 옮겨 보세요.

(1) Sit down.
(2) Stop talking.
(3) Take out your books.
(4) Open your books.
(5) Close your books.
(6) Raise your right hands.

1. A, B 두 사람의 대화를 영어로 크게 말해 보세요.

(1) **A** Excuse me.
    B That's okay.
(2) **A** Hurry up!
    B Wait!
(3) **A** Listen.
    B What?
(4) **A** Be quiet!
    B I'm sorry.
(5) **A** I'm hungry.
    B Me, too.
(6) **A** Ouch!
    B Are you all right?
(7) **A** Oops!
    B What's the matter?
(8) **A** I forgot.
    B Oh, no!
(9) **A** Ouch!
    B Swollen?
(10) **A** Oops!
    B Are you all right?

2. 다음을 영어로 크게 말하면서 행동으로 옮겨 보세요.

(1) Stand up, Min-jae.
(2) Come to the front.
(3) Erase the blackboard.
(4) Bring some chalk.
(5) Write your name on the board.
(6) Go back to your seat.

1. A, B 두 사람의 대화를 영어로 크게 말해 보세요.

(1) **A** Give me that.

B Here you are.
(2) A Are you ready?
   B Not yet.
(3) A Whose turn?
   B My turn.
(4) A Can I?
   B Go ahead.
(5) A Really?
   B Of course.
(6) A We won the baseball game.
   B Congratulations.
(7) A What's up?
   B I feel blue.
(8) A I'm sorry.
   B That's all right.
(9) A What happened?
   B I'm hurt.
(10) A We did it.
   B Congratulations.

2. 다음을 영어로 크게 말하면서 행동으로 옮겨 보세요.
(1) Stand up, Hyun-woo.
(2) Walk to the door.
(3) Open the door and go out.
(4) Go to the teacher's room.
(5) Bring an eraser and some chalk.
(6) Put them on the desk.

44. Review 4　　　　　　　　p. 52

1. A, B 두 사람의 대화를 영어로 크게 말해 보세요.
(1) A You look pale.
   B I've been feeling down lately.
(2) A Can I help you?
   B Leave me alone.

(3) A Stand up.
   B Who?
(4) A I don't like it.
   B Me, neither.
(5) A I have a cold.
   B That's too bad.
(6) A I feel dizzy.
   B Since when?
(7) A I don't feel like trying again.
   B Cheer up!
(8) A Come on. Let's go together.
   B That's great.
(9) A Look. It's bleeding.
   B Stay calm. It's not serious.
(10) A Come here.
    B Ji-min?

2. 다음을 영어로 크게 말하면서 행동으로 옮겨 보세요.
(1) Come to the blackboard.
(2) Draw an apple on the board.
(3) Write the words 'an apple' under the picture.
(4) Read the words aloud three times.
(5) Erase the picture and the words.
(6) Go back to your seat and sit down.

55. Review 5　　　　　　　　p. 63

1. A, B 두 사람의 대화를 영어로 크게 말해 보세요.
(1) A Is this a map?
   B Yes, it is.
(2) A Is that a desk?
   B No, it isn't. It's a table.
(3) A Are you a student?
   B Yes, I am.

(4) **A** Are you a doctor?

B No, I'm not. I'm a teacher.

(5) **A** Do you have a cap?

B Yes, I do.

(6) **A** Does he study English?

B No, he doesn't. He studies Chinese.

(7) **A** Can you speak Korean?

B Yes, I can.

(8) **A** Will you open the door?

B Yes, I will.

(9) **A** Will you bring me the bag?

B No, I won't.

(10) **A** Will you open the window?

B Yes, of course.

2. 다음을 영어로 크게 말하면서 행동으로 옮겨 보세요.

(1) Take out your notebooks.

(2) Write the numbers from one to ten in them.

(3) Count them aloud two times.

(4) Put a circle around the number nine.

(5) Show your notebook to your teacher.

(6) Close your notebooks.

(4) **A** May I have ice cream?

B Yes, you may.

(5) **A** Do I have to learn English?

B Yes, you have to.

(6) **A** Would you like some milk?

B Yes, please.

(7) **A** May I speak to Jane?

B This is Jane speaking.

(8) **A** Hello! I'd like to speak to Hyun-woo.

B He's on another phone. Who's calling, please?

(9) **A** Hello! Can I speak to Min-jae?

B He's out. Call him again later.

(10) **A** Hello. Is this 855-6343?

B Sorry, wrong number.

2. 다음을 영어로 크게 말하면서 행동으로 옮겨 보세요.

(1) Touch your head.

(2) Touch your nose.

(3) Clap your hands three times.

(4) Stomp your foot five times.

(5) Spin around seven times.

(6) Sit down.

66. Review 6　　　　　　p. 74

1. A, B 두 사람의 대화를 영어로 크게 말해 보세요.

(1) **A** Shall I close the window?

B Yes, please.

(2) **A** Shall we meet at eight in the evening?

B Yes, let's meet then.

(3) **A** Shall he bring the bag?

B Yes, let him bring it.

77. Review 7　　　　　　p. 85

1. A, B 두 사람의 대화를 영어로 크게 말해 보세요.

(1) **A** What's this?

B It's a blackboard.

(2) **A** What's your name?

B My name is Eun Kyoung.

(3) **A** Where's your mother?

B My mother's in the kitchen.

(4) **A** Where are you from?
    B I'm from Seoul, Korea.

(5) **A** When's your birthday?
    B My birthday is September 16th.

(6) **A** How's the weather?
    B It's fine.

(7) **A** Why were you absent yesterday?
    B Because I was sick.

(8) **A** What time is it now?
    B It is six o'clock.

(9) **A** What time is it now?
    B It is twelve−thirty.

(10) **A** Where's your father?
    B He's at his office.

2. 다음을 영어로 크게 말하면서 행동으로 옮겨 보세요.
(1) Bring the box.
(2) Open the box.
(3) Take out one apple.
(4) Eat the apple.
(5) Show a big smile.
(6) Go back to your seat and sit down.

(5) **A** Where are they playing the game?
    B They are playing the game in the classroom.

(6) **A** When are you leaving Seoul?
    B I'm leaving Seoul next week.

(7) **A** How many brothers do you have?
    B I have two.

(8) **A** What can I do for you?
    B I'm just looking around.

(9) **A** How much money do you need?
    B I need ten dollars.

(10) **A** When is he arriving here?
    B He's arriving here soon.

2. 다음을 영어로 크게 말하면서 행동으로 옮겨 보세요.
(1) Take this box.
(2) Show me the top of the box.
(3) Touch the bottom of the box.
(4) Open the box.
(5) Show me the inside of the box.
(6) Put the lid down.

88. Review 8   p. 96

1. A, B 두 사람의 대화를 영어로 크게 말해 보세요.
(1) **A** What day is it today?
    B It is Sunday today.

(2) **A** What's the date today?
    B It's September 16th.

(3) **A** How old are you?
    B I'm ten years old.

(4) **A** What are you doing now?
    B I'm reading a story book.

99. Review 9   p. 107

1. A, B 두 사람의 대화를 영어로 크게 말해 보세요.
(1) **A** How does your sister get to school?
    B She goes to school by bus.

(2) **A** Is there a piano in the classroom?
    B Yes, there is.

(3) **A** How many students are there in your class?
    B There are twenty−five students.

(4) **A** What are you going to do tomorrow?

　　B I'm going to make a model airplane.

(5) **A** Would you like to play baseball with us?

　　B Yes, I'd like to.

(6) **A** It's time to go to school.

　　B I have to hurry up.

(7) **A** Where are you going?

　　B I'm going to the library to read some books.

(8) **A** How do you do?

　　B I'm glad to meet you.

(9) **A** It's time to have lunch.

　　B Let's have lunch.

(10) **A** How much water is there in the pool?

　　B There's not much in it.

2. 다음을 영어로 크게 말하면서 행동으로 옮겨 보세요.

(1) Close your books.

(2) Put all of your things in your bags.

(3) Clean your desks.

(4) Stand up.

(5) Say 'Good-bye' to your teacher.

(6) Go out of the classroom and go home.